I0003974

IMPORTANT SITES FOR
KINDLE USERS

The 12 Sites All Kindle Users Must Know

BY

DAVID D. HEDGE

COPYRIGHT©2020

COPYRIGHT

No part of this, publication may be reproduced, distributed, or transmitted in any form or by any means, including photocopy, recording or other electronic or mechanical methods, or by any information storage and retrieval system without the prior written permission of the publisher, except in a case of very brief quotations embodied in critical reviews and certain other noncommercial use per-mitted by copyright law.

Contents

COPYRIGHT..2

CHAPTER 1..4

CHAPTER 1..4

   INTRODUCTION 4

CHAPTER 2..6

   THE 12 SITES ALL KINDLE USERS SHOULD KNOW 6

CHAPTER 3..8

   KINDKINDLE: RESEARCH EBOOKS BY THEIR PRICES........8

CHAPTER 4..10

   BOOKZZ: DOWNLOAD FREE KINDLE EBOOKS ON YOUR KINDLE DEVICE...10

CHAPTER 5..12

   OVERDRIVE: WAYS TO RECEIVE BOOKS FROM PUBLIC LIBRARIES...12

CHAPTER 6..14

   BOOKLENDING: LENDING KINDLE EBOOKS TO OTHER KINDLE USERS...14

CHAPTER 7...16

INSTAPAPER: WAYS TO SEND YOUR ARTICLES TO YOUR
KINDLE 16

CHAPTER 8...17

KINDLE4RSS: RSS FEEDS AND SEND TO YOUR KINDLE...17

CHAPTER 9...18

ONLINE-CONVERT: WAYS TO CONVERT YOUR EBOOK
FORMATS...18

CHAPTER 10...20

BOOKDROP: WAYS TO MAKE USE OF YOUR DROPBOX
AND TRANSFER DOCUMENTS TO IT 20

CHAPTER 11...22

IFTTT: WAYS TO REPLACE THE KINDLE USERS TASKS 22

CHAPTER 12...23

KBOARDS: WAYS TO CONNECT TO YOUR ONLINE
FORUM FOR OTHER KINDLE USERS 23

CHAPTER 13...25

/r/KINDLE: SUBREDDIT TO OTHER KINDLE OWNERS....25

CHAPTER 14...26

KINDLE ANNALS: PODCAST TO OTHR KINDLE OWNERS 26

CHAPTER 15..27

MORE VITAL INFORMATION ABOUT KINDLE YOU NEED
TO KNOW..27

THE END 28

CHAPTER 1

INTRODUCTION

Most people limit themselves and their devices because they do not know the usefulness and other side benefits of the kindle fire. They therefore use it only as E-reader, therefore depriving them of other beautiful advantages and benefits of the Amazon Kindle Fire device.

The Kindle is one of the world most popular android tablets from Amazon, own by more than 3 million users, with the amazing features in it.

This book (guide) is designed to show you twelve (12) significant sites that will be of invaluable benefit to all Kindle users.

The Kindle is selling beyond expectations and many persons who have followed previous instructions have testified to this amazing device just by following these instructions carefully.

Once you try it, you too will testify as most people all over the world haven't gotten the opportunity to know different sites as a Kindle owner, but dis book gives the breakdown of all solution to any problem you might encounter.

Thankfully each step is very easy and simple to follow, that even a beginner can master it in a few minutes.

CHAPTER 2

THE 12 SITES ALL KINDLE USERS SHOULD KNOW

Kindles are out of this world. In fact, there are people who once didn't fancy the idea of a kindle Fire device for just E-book but became interested when they read guides like this and tried one. Beautiful as kindle fire devices are there are a number of third-party sites that will be handing if you must enjoy your Kindle Fire device.

If you are yet to have this amazing device, maybe you should consider it for these reasons:

1.) E-readers are bigger and easier on the eyes.

2.) They have relatively stronger battery lives than most Smartphone and tablets.

3.) It's a much easier way to carry around lots of books anywhere you go.

4.) Kindle can assist you read more books in lesser time.

If you have intention to get one, here are some tips: There are diverse models to pick and make your choice from, and they are all good. Note though, that you can also read Kindle eBooks even when you don't a Kindle device. These sites can be useful to know even when you don't have a Kindle fire device proper.

CHAPTER 3

KINDKINDLE: RESEARCH EBOOKS BY THEIR PRICES

One difficult part of the Kindle Store (including Amazon products widely) is the interface. Browsing can be discouraging sometimes uninteresting and it can make finding the Kindle Store so unexciting.

This is therefore one of the reasons why KindKindle is an advantageous site to know. This known search engine is not only efficient but also has fast filters that enable you search by max price: Free, <$1, <$2, <$5, <$10, and <$20.

Note: They are no other known filter options so you must be smart with your question or inquiry. But it works well.

CHAPTER 4

BOOKZZ: DOWNLOAD FREE KINDLE EBOOKS ON YOUR KINDLE DEVICE

Among other known sites used for searching for free Kindle eBooks, this seems to be the best. It has an intolerable interface sometimes, which can be said to be disadvantageous, but the size of its massive library makes it incomparable. As at the time of writing this guide, you will be able to find close to 2.8 million titles here for free.

BookZZ have a cataloged section for scientific articles. Note once more that the interface can be confusing so you must be smart with your search questions to find the specific article you need. As at the time of writing this guide, you can search for over 52 million free articles. This site is a very important for free Kindle content.

CHAPTER 5

OVERDRIVE: WAYS TO RECEIVE BOOKS FROM PUBLIC LIBRARIES

The Overdrive site is a compilation of eBooks accessible by the public. From there, you can take a look at samples of any title; note though that a library card will be looked-for in order to validate one out to your Kindle. As at the time of this write up, the lending duration by default for an eBook is 21 days.

It's good to know that the Overdrive contains and provides audio books as well. Audio books are different from podcasts, but those who prefer podcast will experience as much satisfaction with audio books because the benefits are almost the same: as you can engage in other activities like driving and reading while listening to amazing piece. Note: Audio books are relatively more expensive, so, save money instead by lending from the library.

CHAPTER 6

BOOKLENDING: LENDING KINDLE EBOOKS TO OTHER KINDLE USERS

BookLending is an astounding service that complements Overdrive. Despite the fact that, lending from a general library (one directional) refers to Overdrive. Whereas BookLending present the general public or group of users who contribute eBooks among themselves (two directional).

As a participant, you can put up your eBooks to lend and decide to lend the eBooks that others have put up. However, you won't be able to read eBooks while they are on loan to others, and a characteristic loan period can last between 14 to 21 days.

Note: eBook lending is an Amazon feature, as such there won't be any risk in participating in booklending, as it only match borrowers with lenders.

CHAPTER 7

INSTAPAPER: WAYS TO SEND YOUR ARTICLES TO YOUR KINDLE

Instapaper is a relatively easy service that enables you save web articles in a place, making it possible for you read through them all at once when you have the time. It has other interesting features, like allowing you distribute those articles among others or send them to be read on other devices.

As a Kindle user, Instapaper is very useful, as it can be set to from time to time send your articles over to your Kindle device in a format that enables you read it (e.g. clean font, no ads etc.). For you therefore to browse the web, you

have to as well save articles for later, and
awake to your article-filled Kindle –
fundamentally a morning newspaper.

CHAPTER 8

KINDLE4RSS: RSS FEEDS AND SEND TO YOUR KINDLE

Some years ago, Kindle Feeder became popular because it allowed persons to set up various RSS feeds that would be summed, converted into an "e-periodical" eBook, and send to your Kindle device every night.

Kindle4RSS is similar but not a famous or widely-spread alternative that provide the same primary reason.

You firstly set up a group of RSS feeds, which will be subsequently auto-delivered to your device daily with a "Table of Content" and making browsing easier. All published images are integrated in the library, and it also can alter partial-text feeds into full text. Everything happens most conveniently.

CHAPTER 9

ONLINE-CONVERT: WAYS TO CONVERT YOUR EBOOK FORMATS

You must note that all eBook formats are of different grades, and not every eBooks are produced in same formats. Suppose you come across a free offer for a highly-expected novel that can be set up in LIT or FB2 format, or maybe you have an older model of Kindle that is unable to read a newer Kindle format. This is when you need to turn to a converter for assistance.

Online-convert is not the only way to do this, but as it's, the most unswerving online solution available. Its supported formats include AZW3, MOBI, EPUB, PDP, FB2, LIT, and more. The converters can change files from one supported format to another. If you pick a desktop substitute, caliber does well converting and managing eBooks.

CHAPTER 10

BOOKDROP: WAYS TO MAKE USE OF YOUR DROPBOX AND TRANSFER DOCUMENTS TO IT

If you usually procure and/or get your eBooks straight on your Kindle device, know that you don't need this device. If you do not use Dropbox at all, then this service isn't for you either. If you nonetheless prefer to acquire/get by using your PC and you use Dropbox regularly, then this is interesting and helpful.

BookDrop is a colossal time-saver that lets you send books from your PC straight to your Kindle using a difficult action of 'drag-and-drop' eBooks into a precise folder on your

Dropbox account. In case the folder is made public, friends can send you eBooks by dropping into it.

One beautiful thing is that BookDrop supports EPUB, CBZ, and CBR files, which will be converted into a Kindle-supported format by design before being sent to your device.

CHAPTER 11

IFTTT: WAYS TO REPLACE THE KINDLE USERS TASKS

IFTTT is an automatic service that allows you set up "triggers" and get them connected with "actions" that are performed any time the given trigger occurs. For example, with this IFTTT recipe, any feed article tagged as "Kindle" will be sent to your device automatically.

You can search the IFTTT site for already existing recipes, but it's more efficient and cooperative if you can create your own recipes. Since the site supports thousands of varying triggers and actions, your mind and fakeness are the only limitations you may have.

CHAPTER 12

KBOARDS: WAYS TO CONNECT TO YOUR ONLINE FORUM FOR OTHER KINDLE USERS

It might interest you to know that thousands of Kindle users check into KBoards daily to discuss all manner of Kindle-related topics. You will nonetheless find subsections especially dedicated to some specific devices (e.g. Kindle Fire), dedicated activities (e.g. publishing Kindle eBooks), and reading/discovering new Kindle eBooks to enjoy.

I'm interested in the segment that deals with trading devices, searching deals and discounts on eBooks, device reviews, and most significantly the section on Kindle tips and tricks.

CHAPTER 13

/r/KINDLE: SUBREDDIT TO OTHER KINDLE OWNERS

For those who do not enjoy Reddit, feel free to turn-over. Reddit is among Top 25 website in terms of global traffic; whenever you are feeling like associating with an active online community, it should be your first stop. As at the time of this write up, /r/Kindle has above 31,000 subscribers worldwide and hundreds of new thread daily.

Most of these new threads are support request; but the subreddit can be as well a great way to keep on top of news concerning Kindle and appraisals for new devices, special links to deals, and a monthly "What Are You

Reading?" thread that might take you to some captivating new read for you.

CHAPTER 14

KINDLE ANNALS: PODCAST TO OTHR KINDLE OWNERS

The Kindle Chronicles podcast has been in existence since 2008 and this beats any other podcast, more so when the topic is a important as kindle. In every episode there is a guest with whom the host talks about different topics that are related to Kindles, e-readers, eBooks, tips, Amazon, and more.

Subsequent episodes are however not so Kindle-focused anymore, but you can always go into the podcast's archives and listen only to those you think meaningful.

Are you searching for something like Kindle Chronicles but attention are on the books instead of reading devices? Check out our compilation of beautiful podcasts for reading devices.

CHAPTER 15

MORE VITAL INFORMATION ABOUT KINDLE YOU NEED TO KNOW

If you have additional enquiries about these sites, should check out these enormous tips for taking charge of your Kindle. Some features like 'Kindle First' will demand an Amazon Prime subscription, but not all do. Example of such is Kindle Unlimited.

Do well to check these frequent Kindle issues and solutions with this scarce Kindle knowledge you probably didn't know about. Put all of these in a box and you will be in charge of your kindle device in no time.

THE END

www.ingramcontent.com/pod-product-compliance
Lightning Source LLC
LaVergne TN
LVHW041222050326
832903LV00021B/747